Selected poems

After Every Green Thing (poems)
Walking Under Water (poems)
Ash on a Young Man's Sleeve
Some Corner of an English Field
Tenants of the House (poems)
Poems, Golders Green (poems)
Modern European Verse (ed.)
Three Questor Plays
Medicine on Trial
A Small Desperation (poems)

Selected poems:

DANNIE ABSE

NEW YORK
OXFORD UNIVERSITY PRESS
1970

Contents

[v]

A small desperation—1968

Early poems

The uninvited

They came into our lives unasked for.
There was light momentarily, a flicker of wings,
a dance, a voice, and then they went out
again, like a light, leaving us not so much
in darkness, but in a different place
and alone as never before.

So we have been changed
and our vision no longer what it was,
and our hopes no longer what they were;
so a piece of us has gone out with them also,
a cold dream subtracted without malice,

the weight of another world added also,
and we did not ask, we did not ask ever
for those who stood smiling
and with flowers before the open door.

We did not beckon them in, they came in uninvited,
the sunset pouring from their shoulders,
so they walked through us as they would through water,
and we are here, in a different place,
changed and incredibly alone,
and we did not know, we do not know ever.

Roots

A man with no roots is lost
like the darkness in the forest.
Heart, my heart, what red voices cry
centuries of suffering in my flowing hands?

Love lasts as long as there are
two people, however silent the word.
Love, my love, how may I meet your eyes,
how may I meet the eyes that I will close?

Future, my future, on whose arms
will my hands be planted?
Love, my love, be assured your eyes
will live after you like children.

Epithalamion

Singing, today I married my white girl
beautiful in a barley field.
Green on thy finger a grass blade curled,
so with this ring I thee wed, I thee wed,
and send our love to the loveless world
of all the living and all the dead.

Now, no more than vulnerable human,
we, more than one, less than two,
are nearly ourselves in a barley field—
and only love is the rent that's due
though the bailiffs of time return anew
to all the living but not the dead.

Shipwrecked, the sun sinks down harbours
of a sky, unloads its liquid cargoes
of marigolds, and I and my white girl
lie still in the barley—who else wishes
to speak, what more can be said
by all the living against all the dead?

Come then all you wedding guests:
green ghost of trees, gold of barley,
you blackbird priests in the field,
you wind that shakes the pansy head
fluttering on a stalk like a butterfly;
come the living and come the dead.

Listen flowers, birds, winds, worlds,
tell all today that I married
more than a white girl in the barley—
for today I took to my human bed
flower and bird and wind and world,
and all the living and all the dead.

Letter to Alex Comfort

Alex, perhaps a colour of which neither of us had dreamt
may appear in the test-tube with God knows what
   admonition.
Ehrlich, certainly, was one who broke down the mental
   doors,
yet only after his six hundred and sixth attempt.

Koch also, painfully, and with true German thoroughness,
eliminated the impossible to prove that too many of us
are dying from the same disease. Visible, on the slide
at last—Death—and the thin bacilli of an ancient distress.

Still I, myself, don't like Germans, but prefer the unkempt
voyagers who, like butterflies drunk with suns,
can only totter crookedly in the dazed air
to reach, charmingly, their destination as if by accident.

That Greek one, then, is my hero who watched the bath
   water
rise above his navel, and rushed out naked, 'I found it,
I found it' into the street in all his shining and forgot
that others would only stare at his genitals.
   What laughter!

Or Newton, leaning in Woolsthorpe against the garden
   wall,
forgot his indigestion and all such trivialities,
but gaped up at heaven in just surprise, and, with
true gravity, witnessed the vertical apple fall.

O what a marvellous observation! Who would have
   reckoned
that such a pedestrian miracle could alter history,
that, henceforward, everyone must fall, whatever
their rank, at thirty-two feet per second, per second?

You too, I know, have waited for doors to fly open, played
with your cold chemicals, written long letters
to the Press; listened to the truth afraid, and dug deep
into the wriggling earth for a rainbow with an honest spade.

But nothing rises. Neither spectres, nor oil, nor love.
And the old professor must think you mad, Alex, as you
   rehearse
poems in the laboratory like vows, and curse those
   clever scientists
who dissect away the wings and haggard heart from the
   dove.

Tenants of the house—1957

Leaving Cardiff

I wait in the evening air.
Sea-birds drop down to the sea.
I prepare to sail from where
the docks' derelictions are.

I stand on the deck and stare,
slack hammocks of waves below,
while black shapes upon the pier
make the furthest star seem near.

Now the funnel's negations blow
and my eyes, like spaces, fill,
and the knots of water flow,
pump to my eyes and spill.

For what *who* would choose to go
when *who* sailing made no choice?
Not for one second, I know,
can I be the same man twice.

The straw coloured flames flare still,
spokes over the long horizon,
and the boats under the hill
of Penarth, unload and move on.

Letter to *The Times*

Sir, I have various complaints to make.
The roses, first. When they are ripped
from the earth expiring, we sigh for them,
prescribe tap-water, aspirin, and salt.
But when we lie down under the same earth,
in a dry silly box, do they revive us?
Their odour of rose-ghosts does not change
at all, and they continue to call out
in their red and white morse the old, old
messages as if nothing had happened. Again,
consider trees. My God, the impresario
trees. Just try, Sir, just try to cut one down
in Fitzjohn's Avenue at three o'clock
in the ordinary afternoon. You will be
prosecuted. Soon the Householders will arrange
themselves into a deranged *mob*. They'll grow
Hitler moustaches, Mussolini chins. Frightful,
and write oathy letters to the Council,
naming you *tree-criminal*. Yet tell me, when
the bombs met their shadows in London,
amidst the ruins of voices, did one tree, just one
tree write an angry note in its sly green ink?
No, they only dropped faded tears in autumn
selfishly thinking of their own hamadryads . . .
BUSINESS AS USUAL was, and is, their trite
slogan. Away then with trees and roses.
They are inhuman. Away also with rivers:
the disgusting Ganges bleeding from Brahma's
big toe; the Rubicon cause of a Civil War;
the Acheron, River of Sorrows—Tiber that drowned
Horatius the One-Eyed, the sweating Rhone,
Rhine, Don, and the vulgar Volga, not to

mention the garrulous Mississippi with its
blatant river-smell. Even the English
rivers can do no more than reflect inverted
values, turn chaste swans upside down
like so many flies on the roof of the waters.
Swans, however, *cannot* swim upside down.
At least, I have never seen them. Is this distortion
of truth deliberate? Has ever one river,
one river, Sir, written eulogies of waterfalls
to plead for the reprieve of Mankind? And stars,
so indifferent and delinquent, stars which we have
decorated with glittering adjectives more numerous
than those bestowed on Helen's eyes—do they
warn us when they fall? Not a hint.
Not a star-wink. They are even too lazy
to shine when we are most awake. Creatures
of Night, they are probably up to amoral
purposes. You can't trust a star, that's sure.
So when the greenfly is in the rose,
and the dragonfly drops its shadow in the river:
when the axe hides in the tree with its listening
shriek, and clouds gag the starlight
with grey handkerchiefs—I contend, Sir,
that we should pity them no more,
but concern ourselves with more natural things.

Verses at night

Sleepless, by the windowpane I stare—
  black aeroplanes disturb the air.
    The ticking moon glares down aghast.
    The seven branched tree is bare.

Oh how much like Europe's gothic Past!
  This scene my nightmare's metaphrast:
  glow of the radioactive worm,
    the preterites of the Blast.

Unreal? East and West fat Neros yearn
  for other fiddled Romes to burn;
  and so dogma cancels dogma
    and heretics in their turn.

By my wife now, I lie quiet as a
  thought of how moon and stars might blur,
  and miles of smoke squirm overhead
    rising to Man's arbiter;

the grey skin shrivelling from the head,
  our two skulls in the double bed,
  leukaemia in the soul of all
    flowing through the blood instead.

'No,' I shout, as by her side I sprawl,
  'No,' again, as I hear my small,
  dear daughter whimper in her cot,
    and across the darkness call.

The second coming

The ground twitches and the noble head
(so often painted) breaks through the cracked crust,
hair first, then ivory forehead into the sunlit field;
the earth yields silently to the straining.
A blackbird flies away.

The eyes open suddenly
just above the grass, seeing corn. No man is near.
Sound of days of heat, of silence.
It is lonely to be born.
And now he's breathing—air not earth
who inhaled worms and death so long.

Still his body in darkness, lightward pushing.
Pause, rest, he is tired now, enough to delight
in looking. Is this true: the world all heaven,
head in corn, with pale butterflies
staggering over him?

He cannot rise further.
The earth is heavy on his shoulders.
Cry out, shout, oh help is near.
Dangerously, the machine passes scything corn,
but the driver does not hear, cannot hear
—and now that noble head is gone,
a liquid redness in the yellow
where the mouth had been.

Dig, I say dig, you'll
find arms, loins, white legs, to prove my story—
and one red poppy in the corn.

The victim of Aulis

A multitude of masts in the harbour.
The sails limp in the air, becalmed.
   The tired sea barely moving.
The sea breathes quietly, Agamemnon.
   The wind is dead.
The sunlight licking the waters,
the waters lapping at the boats.
   Heat haze.
The King prowls the still deck
back and fore, while the Captains quarrel.
We only throw dice and curse.
   The child! The child!
The whisper of the sea, the secret of the sea,
the sea is dreaming and a tall slave sings.
   What are we to do?
They will think of a way, we have had nothing
of education, we must obey, being little men.
   The cause is just.
     Leave it to the Captains.
       What does Calchas say?
   The child! The child!
And they, thinking of their own daughters
with clumsy father-pride, though those
other virgins are faceless now, indistinct
as the mingling of voices, as the shuffle of the sea,
the little sound of the sea.
   It has been a long time.
     Leave it to the priests.
       Conference at Aulis.
And he, the King, listening to the whisper of Calchas,
to the sea restless in its sleep while a tall slave sings—
sings of home and alien distances, a slow voice, sad

as a light, as a flame burning in daytime.
   Agamemnon is in religion.
     It's that or nothing now.
       The child! The child!
And she peering down through the fathomless minds
of the sea, at the green shadows and dark dreams of fish—
for the deep thoughts of the sea are fish—
and she trailing her small hands in the waters
playing with coloured beads of spray.
   Come with me.
    Why father?
We sit on the stone quay with the sun and the seagulls.
We know nothing of rough mythologies, only fact.
We need the gods more than they need us.
   And never will some home again.
Artemis is offended, Calchas said,
staring at golden bangles spinning on the sea,
at arrows of poisoned sunlight pricking the flat sea;
the yellow masts vertical, pointing at the blue, luxurious sky,
the white sails lagging down, without life, without wind.
   Calchas mumbles: Troy, Troy.
We only throw dice and curse the day we sailed away,
grumble and tell tall tales of faithless women,
remembering Helen ravished in a foreign bed.
   The child! The child!
And the King musing: what will her mother say?
The sigh and the sadness of it. And she who has no breasts
trailing her small hands in the waters, just a child,
still a child—that is a fearful thing.
   Come with me.
    Why father?
     Murder at Aulis.

Oh the questions of the young-to-be-slain,
and the memory of black eyelashes pulled apart suddenly
revealing more white of the eye than a man bargained for.
  The King is in religion
   whose name is great among the Greeks—
the blood, ridiculously crimson, in the groves of Artemis,
and the wind howling, why father? why father?
for many days and louder in the silence of the night,
and dispossessed and possessing him in the mornings,
in the sea-spray climbing, and in the sea-howl,
as the fleet drags on aslant in the furious wind.
  They thought of a way.
   We are little men
     who follow and obey
as the cracked sails billow out half below the leaping sea,
as the tall slave sings why Father? why Father?

The moment

You raise your eyes from the level book
as if deeply listening. You are further than I call.
Like Eurydice you wear a hurt and absent look,
but I'm gentle for the silence into which you fall so sadly.
What are you thinking? Do you love me?
Suddenly you are not you at all but a ghost
dreaming of a castle to haunt or a heavy garden;
some place eerie, and far from me. But now a door
is banging outside, so you turn your head surprised.

You speak my name and someone else has died.

Poem and message

Out on the tormented, midnight sea
your sails are blown in jeopardy.
Gales of grief and terrors force
you from the spirit's chartered course.

But, in the storm, lighthouses mark
rocks of dangers in the dark;
so from this shore of cold I write
tiny flashes in the night.

Words of safety, words of love,
a beacon in the dark to save
you from the catastrophic sea,
and navigate you home to me.

Dear, vague as a distant star, I,
in the huge night's amorphous lie,
find one small and luminous truth
of which our usual love was proof.

And I call your name as loud I can
and give you all the light I am.

Anniversary

The tree grows down from a bird.
The strong grass pulls up the earth
to a hill. Wade here, my dear,
through green shallows of daisies.
I hear the voice talking that is dead
behind the voice that is talking now.
The clocks of the smoky town
strike a quiet, grating sound.
Tomorrow will be the same.
Two sit on this hill and count
two moving from the two that stayed.

What happens to a flame blown out?
What perishes? Not this view,
nor my magnified hand in yours
whatever hurt and angers done.
I breathe in air the dead breathed out.
When first you inclined your face
to mine, my sweet ally came,
with your brown eyes purely wide.
My right hand on your left breast
I said, I have little to tell my dear.
For the pure bird, a pure cage.

Oh the silence that you lost
blind in the pandemonium
of the kiss and ruined was.
My dear, my dear, what perishes?
I hear this voice in a voice to come.

Looking at a map

The map does not show the rain:
only pale blue for sea and Great Britain
a mosaic of multi-coloured counties
where the English weather never changes,
and the local hills and mountain ranges
are shaded heavily—though never white
   as moods of snow may shade them.

Clouds never shamble over
unless this cigarette-smoke I blow out
be cloud: this sad electric bulb be sun
where constellations of flies (not planets)
   all silently swing about.

False! False! Boring lines squiggle,
meaning empty roads, hedges and wet tyres,
or desolation of damp railway lines
where no one encounters a red lamp danger.
   But there's menace of a kind.
Why else do official cartographers
   condemn the whole land behind
a strict cage emptied of noughts and crosses
where no happy latitude is given?

And this, too, another lie:
this measurement of a lifetime's journey
in inches, these little, exact circles
for names of places where untamed people
   privately hide and love and cry.

Enough, I switch off the electric bulb,
   the thin current of the sun.
Oh nightly, something secret breathes and moves;
   the whole flat, civilised map
that here is cracked into coloured counties,
   like energy explodes, goes black;
   these names of cities break out
into dotty, shifting points of glitterings,
   and the light blue tide flows back.

On hearing the monologue of a deaf poet
For David Wright

People always depart, always say 'goodbye'.
You swear you can *hear* their changing faces.
I listen to careful words that falsify,
and the sincere sound of 'alas' disgraces
all purity of promises. Words die

in the air—but not on scraps of paper
that you, afflicted, could easily hoard:
snapshots of conversation fixed forever.
Ink endures, not the aural record,
not even the delirium of love's fever.

So bless the four senses that make the fifth
accept what it chooses, that may ignore
or disguise the abuse: the nameless width
of injuries, the unmitigated store
of insults, loud and authoritative.

Yet curse not the ear lightly as I do
who have the gift of hearing. I would fear
the continual sound of snow that falls on snow.
Those profound, sad silences that I hear
are enough between voices that are true.

I, like you, would rather know the shocked cries
of the animals, my child's unnecessary scream,
and praise the divine for verbal pain and lies.
Better this, than mouths moving in a dream
of the deaf where no one protests or sighs.

Though you hear very well not having heard.
And I, on this page, need write no message,
no keyless note from my clamorous world,
for doors open with the din of the image
to make audible every terrible word.

Duality

Twice upon a time,
there was a man who had two faces,
two faces but one profile:
not Jekyll and Hyde, not good and bad,
and if one were cut, the other would bleed—
two faces different as hot and cold.

At night, hung on the hooks on the wall
above that man's minatory head,
one wants brass where one wants gold,
one sees white and one sees black,
and one mouth eats the other
until the second sweet mouth bites back.

They dream their separate dreams
hanging on the wall above the bed.
The first voice cries: 'He's not what he seems,'
but the second one sighs: 'He is what he is,'
then one shouts 'wine' and the other screams 'bread',
and so they will all his raving days
until they die on his double-crossed head.

At signposts he must wear them both.
Each would go their separate ways
as the East or the West wind blows—
and dark and light they both would praise,
but one would melt, the other one freeze.

I am that man twice upon this time:
my two voices sing to make one rhyme.
Death I love and Death I hate,
(I'll be with you soon and late).
Love I love and Love I loathe,
God I mock and God I prove,
yes, myself I kill, myself I save.

Now, now, I hang these masks on the wall.
Oh Christ, take one and leave me all
lest four tears from two eyes fall.

The trial

The heads around the table disagree,
some say hang him from the gallows tree.

Some say high and some say low
to swing, swing, swing, when the free winds blow.

I wanted to be myself, no more,
so I screwed off the face that I always wore,

I pulled out the nails one by one—
I'd have given that face to anyone.

For those vile features were hardly mine;
to wear another's face is a spiritual crime.

Why, imagine the night when I would wed
to kiss with wrong lips in the bridal bed . . .

But now the crowd screams loud in mockery:
oh string him up from the gallows tree.

Silence! the Judge commands, or I'll clear the court,
to hang a man up is not a sport—

though some say high and some say low
to swing, swing, swing, when the free winds blow.

Prisoner, allow me once more to ask:
what did you do with your own pure mask?

I told you, your honour, I threw it away,
it was only made of skin-coloured clay.

A face is a man, a bald juryman cries,
for one face lost, another man dies.

Gentlemen, this citizen we daren't acquit
until we know what he did with it.

It was only a face, your honour, that I lost;
how much can such a sad thing cost?

A mask is a lifetime, my bad man,
to replace such a gift nobody can.

Consider the case of that jovial swan
who took a god's face off to put a bird's face on

and Leda swooning by the side of the sea
and the swan's eyes closed in lechery.

No! No! your honour, my aim was just—
I did what every true man must.

Quiet, prisoner! Why I remember a priest remark
that he picked up a dog's face in the dark,

then he got as drunk as a man can be
and barked at God in blasphemy.

But it was a human face, sir, I cast away;
for that offence do I have to pay?

The heads around the table disagree,
some say hang him from the gallows tree.

Some say high and some say low
to swing, swing, swing, when the free winds blow.

At the back of the courtroom quietly stand
his father and mother hand-in-hand.

They can't understand the point of this case
or why he discarded his own dear face.

But it's not *my* face, father, he had said,
I don't want to die in a strange, wrong bed.

Look in the mirror, mother, stare in deep;
is that mask your own, yours to keep?

The mirror is oblong, the clock is round,
all our wax faces go underground.

Once, I built a bridge right into myself
to ransack my soul for invisible wealth

and, afterwards, I tore off my mask because
I found not the person I thought I was.

With the wrong mask, another man's life I live—
I must seek my own face, find my own grave.

The heads around the table disagree,
some say hang him from the gallows tree.

Some say high and some say low
to swing, swing, swing, when the free winds blow.

I'll sum up, the severe Judge moans,
showing the white of his knucklebones.

What is a face but the thing that you see,
the symbol and fate of identity?

How would we recognise each from each:
a dog from a man—which face on a leash?

And when tears fall where no face is,
will the tears be mine or will they be his?

To select hot coal or gold no man is free,
each choice being determined by identity.

But exchange your face then what you choose
is gained, like love, by what you lose.

Now you twelve jurymen please retire,
put your right hands in ice and your left in fire.

A hole where the face was, frightens us,
and a man who can choose is dangerous.

So what is your verdict going to be,
should he be hung from a gallows tree?

Oh some say high and some say low
to swing, swing, swing, when the free winds blow.

The meeting

Where has the Speaker been all these years?
Rinse your eyes from gardens, follow the railway lines.
Come nearer to the dream in the halls of mean cities.
Enter, imagine, listen: the cry down the flight
of stairs, the squeak of chairs, a floor without
carpets; as of old, on Babel, murmur of many languages.
But one dream.

　　Stroll then to the eternal meeting through streets
tangled like string, walk over square shadows of shops,
dark shops that sell only a synthetic dream, cross under
the hoardings of advertisements. Melancholy spring,
springtime, dust, petrol, blossoms of carbon monoxide.
Here, here, in the backstreets of any city, the one dream.
There, there, past the beggar and war victim,
past these public refusals, past the depots and warehouses,
past the public urinals, nearer to the dead cat
laid out in the gutter, go to the entrance of the seedy hall
and note the writing on the wall.
Far from the chessboard fields where cows and horses munch
sunlight, far from the factories of grass and the trees'
workshops for artificial limbs
　　the afternoon stretches and stretches past railway
bridges, cranes, chimney pots, canals—until it breaks
with the sound of the hooter, break into eyes of electricity
sad behind windows, falling off lampposts. And in
the juke-box dark, the newsboys crying the world's
　　testament:
'Riots. Police fire on mobs. Tearing of treaties.'
Moon over patched rooftops, glinting on railway lines
always going away from.

Far from the horses and cows munching starlight,
go to the heartbroken hall. Remember the hand
that wrote the writing on the wall.
Babel, one dream, discontent of voices.

Arrive at the meeting down a flight of stairs:
regard the glass of water on the table, the rows of empty
    chairs.
Whispering voices and a deaf man asking,
What are they saying, what are they saying?
And the traffic outside and a clock striking the time
    outside.
They are not saying anything, sir. The Speaker has not
    arrived.
One day our hands will fall: read the writing on the wall.
Far away the conscripted dead, the scarecrow in the dark
field, like an artificial ragged ghost.
But here—the shuffle of feet, the table, the platform,
the tatty banners, the chairman staring straight ahead,
both hands behind his head, waiting for the unknown
Speaker.
And lights flickering Exit, Exit, Exit.

Night. Moonshine on rooftops, pegs on empty washing lines,
barking of dogs, blue television light behind curtains,
whimper of a distant locomotive like a child's impotent cry.
Discontent of voices. One dream.
The eternal meeting and exit exit exit exit.
Still the audience waits for the Speaker,
here, everywhere, forever—waits in the dim hall,
watching an x-rayed hand scrawling on the wall,
waits, waits, with a yawn, a crossing of legs, and a cough.

The game

Follow the crowds to where the turnstiles click.
The terraces fill. *Hoompa*, blares the brassy band.
Saturday afternoon has come to Ninian Park
and, beyond the goal posts, in the Canton Stand
between black spaces, a hundred matches spark.

Waiting, we recall records, legendary scores:
Fred Keenor, Hardy, in a royal blue shirt.
The very names, sad as the old songs, open doors
before our time where someone else was hurt.
Now, like an injured beast, the great crowd roars.

The coin is spun. Here all is simplified,
and we are partisan who cheer the Good,
hiss at passing Evil. Was Lucifer offside?
A wing falls down when cherubs howl for blood.
Demons have agents: the Referee is bribed.

The white ball smacked the crossbar. Satan rose
higher than the others in the smoked brown gloom
to sink on grass in a ballet dancer's pose.
Again, it seems, we hear a familiar tune
not quite identifiable. A distant whistle blows.

Memory of faded games, the discarded years;
talk of Aston Villa, Orient, and the Swans.
Half-time, the band played the same military airs
as when the Bluebirds once were champions.
Round touchlines the same cripples in their chairs.

Mephistopheles had his joke. The honest team
dribbles ineffectively, no one can be blamed.
Infernal backs tackle, inside forwards scheme,
and if they foul us need we be ashamed?
Heads up! Oh for a Ted Drake, a Dixie Dean.

'Saved' or else, discontents, we are transferred
long decades back, like Faust must pay that fee.
The Night is early. Great phantoms in us stir
as coloured jerseys hover, move diagonally
on the damp turf, and our eidetic visions blur.

God sign our souls! Because the obscure staff
of Hell rule this world, jugular fans guessed
the result halfway through the second half,
and those who know the score just seem depressed.
Small boys swarm the field for an autograph.

Silent the stadium. The crowds have all filed out.
Only the pigeons beneath the roofs remain.
The clean programmes are trampled underfoot,
and natural the dark, appropriate the rain,
whilst, under lamp-posts, threatening newsboys shout.

Poems, Golders Green—1962

The Magician

Off stage, the Great Illusionist owns bad teeth,
cheats at cards, beats his second wife, is lewd;
before studying his art he qualified
as obsessional liar, petty thief.

Transformed by glamorous paraphernalia—
tall top hat, made-up face, four smoking spotlights—
only fellow magicians can sense beneath
that glossy surface, a human failure.

Ready with unseen wires, luminous paint,
with drums and ceremony he fills the stage,
rich twice nightly in his full regalia.
Two extras planted in the audience faint.

Allezup! Closes his eyes, seemingly bored,
and astutely fakes a vulgar miracle,
mutters and reclines to become fakir, saint;
on a hotbed of nails, swallows a sword.

For encore will saw a seedy blonde in half
as music rises to a shrill crescendo;
hacks through wood, skin, vertebrae, spinal cord,
and all except the gods applaud or laugh.

Lord, red blood oozes from the long black box,
oh hocus pocus, oh abracadabra,
whilst, in trumped-up panic, manager and staff
race breathlessly on stage, undo the locks.

Patrons prefer bisected blondes to disappear.
Relieved, commercial men and their average wives
now salaciously prepare for futher shocks,
eagerly yearn to see what they most fear.

Sometimes, something he cannot understand
happens—atavistic powers stray unleashed,
a raving voice he hardly thought to hear,
the ventriloquist's dummy out of hand.

In the box, a vision of himself—and on
those masochistic nails fresh genuine blood,
within his white glove a decomposing hand,
and, unimaginably, his own face gone.

Quite disturbed the disconnected audience boo.
What cheek! This charlatan believes his magic:
not luminous paint across the darkness shone
when, happily, for once, his lies came true.

Or so it seemed. Oh what overbearing pride
if no longer fake but Great Illusionist;
but as phony critics pierce him through and through
he begs for mercy and is justified.

Off stage, that Great Illusionist owns bad teeth,
cheats at cards, beats his second wife, is lewd;
before studying his art he qualified
as obsessional liar, petty thief.

The water diviner

Late, I have come to a parched land
doubting my gift, if gift I have,
the inspiration of water
spilt, swallowed in the sand.

To hear once more water trickle,
to stand in a stretch of silence
the divine pen twisting in the hand:
sign of depths alluvial.

Water owns no permanent shape,
brags, is most itself in chaos;
now, under the shadow of the idol,
dry mouth and dry landscape.

No rain falls with a refreshing sound
to settle tubular in a well,
elliptical in a bowl. No grape
lusciously moulds it round.

Clouds have no constant resemblance
to anything, blown by a hot wind,
flying mirages; the blue background,
light constructions of chance.

To hold back chaos I transformed
amorphous mass: clay, fire, or cloud,
so that the agèd gods might dance
and golden structures form.

I should have built, plain brick on brick,
a water tower. The sun flies on
arid wastes, barren hells too warm,
and me with a hazel stick!

Rivulets vanished in the dust
long ago, great compositions
vaporised, salt on the tongue so thick
that drinking, still I thirst.

Repeated desert, recurring drought,
sometimes hearing water trickle,
sometimes not, I, by doubting first,
believe; believing, doubt.

Red balloon

It sailed across the startled town,
over chapels, over chimney-pots,
wind-blown above a block of flats
before it floated down.

Oddly, it landed where I stood,
and finding's keeping, as you know.
I breathed on it, I polished it,
till it shone like living blood.

It was my shame, it was my joy,
it brought me notoriety.
From all of Wales the rude boys came,
it ceased to be a toy.

I heard the girls of Cardiff sigh
when my balloon, my red balloon,
soared higher like a happiness
towards the dark blue sky.

Nine months since, have I boasted of
my unique, my only precious;
but to no one dare I show it now
however long they swear their love.

'It's a Jew's balloon,' my best friend cried,
'stained with our dear Lord's blood.'
'That I'm a Jew is true,' I said,
said I, 'that cannot be denied.'

'What relevance?' I asked, surprised,
'what's religion to do with this?'
'Your red balloon's a Jew's balloon,
let's get it circumcised.'

Then some boys laughed and some boys cursed,
some unsheathed their dirty knives:
some lunged, some clawed at my balloon,
but still it would not burst.

They bled my nose, they cut my eye,
half conscious in the street I heard,
'Give up, give up your red balloon.'
I don't know exactly why.

Father, bolt the door, turn the key,
lest those sad, brash boys return
to insult my faith and steal
my red balloon from me.

After the release of Ezra Pound

In Jerusalem I asked
the ancient Hebrew poets to forgive you,
and what would Walt Whitman have said
and Thomas Jefferson?   [*Paul Potts*]

In Soho's square mile of unoriginal sin
where the fraudulent neon lights haunt,
but cannot hide, the dinginess of vice,
the jeans and sweater boys spoke of Pound,
and you, Paul, repeated your question.

The chi-chi bums in Torino's laughed and
the virgins of St Martin's School of Art.
The corner spivs with their Maltese masks
loitered for the two o'clock result,
and those in the restaurants of Greek Street,
eating income tax, did not hear the laugh.

Gentle Gentile, you asked the question.
Free now (and we praise this) Pound could answer.

The strip lighting of Soho did not fuse,
no blood trickled from a certain book
down the immaculate shelves of Zwemmer's.
But the circumcised did not laugh.
The swart nudes in the backrooms put on clothes
and the doors of the French pub closed.

Pound did not hear the raw Jewish cry,
the populations committed to the dark
when he muttered through microphones
of murderers. He, not I, must answer.

Because of the structures of a beautiful poet
you ask the man who is less than beautiful,
and wait in the public neurosis of Soho,
in the liberty of loneliness for an answer.

In the beer and espresso bars they talked
of Ezra Pound, excusing the silences of an old man,
saying there is so little time between
the parquet floors of an institution
and the boredom of the final box.

Why, Paul, if that ticking distance between
was merely a journey long enough
to walk the circumference of a Belsen,
Walt Whitman would have been eloquent,
and Thomas Jefferson would have cursed.

Surprise! Surprise!

Talk not of loneliness, but aloneness.
Every thing is alien, everyone strange.
Regard an object closely, our own foot
named, how queer it appears as its toes flex.
Peer at it with greenhorn observation;
thus magnified, what incongruous toenails!
Or the tree outside, we pass every day,
stand below it, stare at it flagrantly
till it becomes uncomfortable, till
its slender boughs, shyly naked beneath
those veined, pellucid leaves, stir a little.
Scrutinised, it grows unrecognisable.
Again, utterly estranged, our colleague
who talks to us on weekdays—just the way
he walks, what a peculiar, indolent
manner of walking, come to think of it;
and lastly, that woman we love fondly,
sounded and labelled, who loves us perhaps,
look how she, while reading the newspaper,
taps her own forehead, checks her cheek, cheekbone,
nose, her martial lip, over and over,
withdrawn in concentration, unaware,
yet feels her face to affirm it's still there.
How then can we whisper, at night, 'My own'?
Oh how everything and everybody
are perplexed and perplexing, deeply unknown.
What surprises is that sometimes we are
not surprised, that a door clicks, half opens,
and we guessed beforehand who would enter.
Is that why we dare to cry: 'I know Smith'?
Now, which of you, suggesting I raise my head
from this page, will call my name familiarly?
You will see, as always, my eyes startled.

The grand view

Mystics, in their far, erotic stance,
neglect our vulgar catastrophes.
I, with cadence, rhyme and assonance,
must pardon their oceanic trance,
their too saintlike immoralities.

For I, too, spellbound by the grand view,
flung through vistas from this windy hill,
am in pure love. I do not know who
it is that I love, but I would flow
into One invisible and still.

Though islanded and inspired by
the merely human, I sing back robes of air
to uncover my ego-plundered eye,
abandoning my apostasy,
no more to make a home out of despair.

Only Moses on the high mountain
at least knew what he was climbing for.
God haunted, wonderstruck, half insane,
that condemned genius brought down again
ten social poems we call the law.

My littleness makes but a private sound,
the little lyric of a little man:
yet, like Moses, I walk on holy ground
since all earth is, and the world is round
I come back to where he began.

My forehead is open. The horns grow out
and exit. Infirm cynics knock inside,
and still ancestral voices shout
visions, visions! Should I turn about
if, by naming all, One is denied?

There are moments when a man must sing
of a lone Presence he cannot see.
To undulations of space I bring
all my love when love is happening:
green directions flying back to me.

There are moments when a man must praise
the astonishment of being alive,
when small mirrors of reality blaze
into miracles: and there's One always
who, by never departing, almost arrives.

After a departure

Intimate god of stations,
on long, faded afternoons
before impatient trains depart,
where the aching lovers wait
and mothers embarrass sons,
discover your natural art;
delicately articulate
an elegy of the heart
for horizons appropriate,
or dialogues for the stage
and the opening of an eye.

Love invents the sadness of
tolerable departures.
So bless every fumbling kiss
when eyes, hands, lips, betray
shy, tentative disclosures,
conclusions that non-lovers miss.
Taxis, buses, surge away
through the grey metropolis
while mortals frown for words to say,
and their ordinary messages
approximate, therefore lie.

Those heroes who departed
spouting famous monologues
were more verbose than we.
Antony at Paddington,
bizarre in his Roman togs,
a sword clanking on his knee,
would have jabbered on and on
love epithets most happily,
well after the train had gone.
Let prosy travellers rage
long as Cleopatras sigh.

Romeo's peroration
for Juliet at Waterloo,
as gulps of steam arise
from the engine on its bit,
and from station-masters too,
would bring tears to the eyes.
Sooty god of stations permit
your express to dally, revise
timetables, dull schedules if it
allows one more classic page
or a Juliet to cry.

Today, I, your professional
pleb of words who must appear
spontaneous, who knows form
to be decorative logic,
whose style is in the error,
ask forgiveness for my storm
of silence when all speech grew sick;
who, waving from the platform,
found even gesture ironic,
afraid of your beautiful coinage
'I love you' and 'Goodbye'.

Two voices

I *A woman to a man*

To own nothing, but to be—
like the vagrant wind that bears
faintest fragrance of the sea
or, in anger, lifts and tears
yet hoards no property;

I praise that state of mind:
wind, music, and you, are such.
All the visible you find
(the invisible you touch)
alter, and leave behind.

To pure being you devote
all your days. You are your eyes,
seemingly near but remote.
Gone, now, the sense of surprise,
like a dying musical note.

Like fragrance, you left no trace,
like anger, you came my way,
like music, you filled the space
(by going, the more you stay).
Departures were in your face.

II *A wife to a husband*

Doth the music always flee?
Who kiss, that they may own,
sing happily, oh happily
of brick on brick till stone
keeps out both wind and sea.

So come back fast, come back slow,
I'll be distance and your home,
every symbol that I know,
church, tower, mosque, and dome,
then by staying, the more you'll go.

Let me breathe in music where
I am nothing but your life;
your designs, directions share,
to be no mistress but a wife,
pluck your meanings from the air.

I'll be all things you would be,
the four winds and the seven seas,
you'll play with such a gaiety
devastating melodies
till music be my body.

Chalk

Chalk, calcium carbonate, should mean school—
a small, neutral stick neither cool nor hot,
its smell should evoke wooden desks slamming
when, squeaking over blackboards, it could not
decently teach us more than one plus one.

Now, no less pedagogic in ruder districts,
on iron railway bridges, where urchins fight,
an urgent scrawl names our failure—BAN THE BOMB,
or more peculiarly, KEEP BRITAIN WHITE.
Chalk, it seems, has some bleeding purposes.

In the night, secretly, they must have come,
strict, clenched men in the street, anonymous,
past closed shops and the sound of running feet
till upstairs, next morning, vacant in a bus,
we observe a once blank wall assaulted.

There's not enough chalk in the wronged world
to spell out one plus one, the perfect lies.
HANDS OFF GUATEMALA—though slogans change,
never the chalk scraping on the pitched noise
of a nerve in violence or in longing.

Return to Cardiff

'Hometown'; well, most admit an affection for a city:
grey, tangled streets I cycled on to school, my first cigarette
in the back lane, and fool, my first botched love affair.
First everything. Faded torments; self-indulgent pity.

The journey to Cardiff seemed less a return than a raid
on mislaid identities. Of course the whole locus smaller:
the mile-wide Taff now a stream, the castle not as in some
    black
gothic dream, but a decent sprawl, a joker's toy façade.

Unfocused voices in the wind, associations, clues,
odds and ends, fringes caught, as when, after the doctor
    quit,
a door opened and I glimpsed the white, enormous face
of my grandfather, suddenly aghast with certain news.

Unable to define anything I can hardly speak,
and still I love the place for what I wanted it to be
as much as for what it unashamedly is
now for me, a city of strangers, alien and bleak.

Unable to communicate I'm easily betrayed,
uneasily diverted by mere sense reflections
like those anchored waterscapes that wander, alter, in the
    Taff,
hour by hour, as light slants down a different shade.

Illusory, too, that lost, dark playground after rain,
the noise of trams, gunshots in what they once called
   Tiger Bay.
Only real this smell of ripe, damp earth when the sun
   comes out,
a mixture of pungencies, half exquisite and half plain.

No sooner than I'd arrived the other Cardiff had gone,
smoke in the memory, these but tinned resemblances,
where the boy I was not and the man I am not
met, hesitated, left double footsteps, then walked on.

Sunday evening

Loved not for themselves those tenors who sing
arias from 'Aida' on horned, tinny
gramophones—but because they take a man back
to a half forgotten thing.

We, transported by this evening loaded
with a song recorded by Caruso,
recall some other place, another time,
now charmingly outmoded.

What, for wrong motives, too often is approved
proves we once existed, becomes mere flattery
—then it's ourselves whom we are listening to,
and, by hearing, we are moved.

To know, haunted, this echo too will fade
with fresh alliteration of the leaves,
as more rain, indistinct, drags down the sky
like a sense of gloom mislaid.

Dear classic, melodic absences
how stringently debarred, kept out of mind,
till some genius on a gramophone
holes defences, breaks all fences.

What lives in a man and calls him back
and back through desolate Sunday evenings?
Indescribable, oh faint generic name:
sweet taste, bitter lack.

The shunters

The colour of grief, and thoroughly tame,
the shunters slave on silver parallels.
Propitious their proletarian numbers.
Only posh expresses sport proper names.

In the tired afternoon drizzle, their smoke
fades into industrial England.
Governed by levers, hearing clanking chains,
how can a smudge of engines run amok?

Rain drags darkness down where shunters work
the blank gloom below hoardings, dejected sheds,
below yellow squares in backs of tenements
whilst, resigned, charcoal trucks clash and jerk.

A prince is due. Like victims shunters wait
meekly—*The Red Dragon*? *The Devon Belle*?
A crash of lights. Four o'clock schoolboys gape
over the bridge, inarticulate.

Later, late, again, far their echoes rage;
hurt, plaintive whistles; hyphenated trucks;
sexual cries from funnels—all punctuate
the night, a despair beyond language.

The French master

Everyone in Class II at the Grammar School
had heard of Walter Bird, known as Wazo.
They said he'd behead each dullard and fool
or, instead, carve off a tail for the fun.

Wazo's cane buzzed like a bee in the air.
Quietly, quietly, in the desks of Form III
sneaky Wazo tweaked our ears and our hair.
Walter Wazo, public enemy No. 1.

Five feet tall, he married sweet Doreen Wall,
and combmarks furrowed his vaselined hair;
his hands still fluttered ridiculously small,
his eyes the colour of a poison bottle.

Who'd think he'd falter, poor love-sick Walter
as bored he read out *Lettres de mon Moulin*;
his mouth had begun to soften and alter,
and Class IV ribbed him as only boys can.

Perhaps through kissing his wife to a moan
had alone changed the shape of his lips,
till the habit of her mouth became his own:
no more Walter Wazo, enemy No. 1.

'Boy', he'd whine, 'yes, please decline the verb to have',
in tones dulcet and mild as a girl.
'Sorry sir, can't sir, must go to the lav,'
whilst Wazo stared out of this world.

Till one day in May Wazo buzzed like a bee
and stung, twice, many a warm, inky hand;
he stormed through the form, a catastrophe,
returned to this world, No. 1.

Alas, alas, to the Vth Form's disgrace
nobody could quote Villon to that villain.
Again the nasty old mouth zipped on his face,
and not a weak-bladdered boy in the class.

Was Doreen being kissed by a Mr. Anon?
Years later, I purred, 'Your dear wife, Mr. Bird?'—
Teeth bared, how he *glared* before stamping on;
and suddenly I felt sorry for the bastard.

Odd

In front of our house in Golders Green
the lawn, like a cliché, mutters 'Rose bushes'.
The whole suburb is very respectable.
Ugly men drive past in funeral suits,
from their necks you can tell they're overweight.

Sodium lamp-posts, at night, hose empty roads
with gold which treacles over pavement trees,
polishes brittle hedges, clings on closed, parked cars.
If a light should fly on in an upstairs room
odds on two someones are going to sleep.

It's unusual to meet a beggar,
you hardly ever see a someone drunk.
It's a nice, clean, quiet, religious place.
For my part, now and then, I want to scream:
thus, by the neighbours, am considered odd.

From the sensible wastes of Golders Green
I journey to Soho where a job owns me.
Soho is not a respectable place.
Underweight women in the gamiest of skirts
bleed a smile of false teeth at ugly men.

Later, the dark is shabby with paste electric
of peeporamas, brothels, clubs and pubs,
restaurants that sport sallow waiters who cough.
If a light should fly on in an upstairs room
odds on two someones are going to bed.

It's customary to see many beggars,
common to meet people roaring and drunk.
It's a nice, loud, dirty, irreligious place.
For my part, now and then, I want to scream:
thus, by Soho friends, am considered odd.

A small desperation—1968

Even

Coffee-time morning, down the gradient,
like a shop window for Jehovah,
they pass my gate to the synagogue
as Saturday skies vault over.

Dressed like that they lose their charm
who carry prayer books, wear a hat.
I don't like them, I don't like them,
and guilty fret—just thinking that.

I don't like them, I don't like them—
again the dodgy thought comes through:
could it be I am another
tormented, anti-semite Jew?

No. Next morning on the Sunday,
processions uphill, piebald, lurch,
in the opposite direction,
towards the ivy-covered church.

Look, dressed for Christ and hygiene,
they glare back like Swiss-Germans
spruced and starched in piety,
and fag on slow as sermons.

All God's robots lose their charm
who carry prayer books, wear a hat.
I don't like them, I don't like them,
and feel less guilty thinking that.

So let both ministers propound
the pathology of religions,
and pass my gate you zealots of
scrubbed, excremental visions.

From a suburban window

Such afternoon glooms, such clouds chimney low—
London, the clouds want to move but can not,
London, the clouds want to rain but can not—
such negatives of a featureless day:
the street empty but for a van passing,
an afternoon smudged by old afternoons.
Soon, despite railings, evening will come
from a great distance trailing evenings.
Meantime, unemployed sadness loiters here.

Quite suddenly, six mourners appear:
a couple together, then three stout men,
then one more, lagging behind, bare-headed.
Not one of the six looks up at the sky,
and not one of them touches the railings.
They walk on and on remembering days,
yet seem content. They employ the décor.
They use this grey inch of eternity,
and the afternoon, so praised, grows distinct.

3 a.m. in the High Street

Outside this church: TRUST IN THE LORD.
Outside that office: SAVE AND PROSPER.
Now, despite the pressures of common sense,
in this High Street before the waking time,
I think Virgil could take me by the hand
past this butcher's shop, and show me, on the hooks,
two live heads, one gnawing at the other.
I think it must be always 3 a.m. in hell.
Listen! The cenotaph clock punishes the hour—
then the strokes of silence like a horror.

The perceptible wind is immortal.
Mourning for no-one, it mourns for everyone,
it blows these damp pavements beneath the bridge
past orange belishas that blink for no-one.
There's nothing beyond but the fabric of night,
there's nothing behind but the cenotaph,
the god of this hour. It seems the tenants
afraid, left hurriedly, forgot switches,
so that occasional shop windows blaze out,
and each lamppost, like an idiot, stares at no-one.

When rain washed cheap green from these traffic lights
the ground smudged. My feet shake off too much noise.
For miles around, neighbouring dogs are muzzled.
Down side-lanes, the houses darkly slumber.
The wind creaks again. Deathly crepitations
from flowered tributes to the cenotaph
on which are carved LOYALTY and JUSTICE.
Look how that god, for Time's sake, unappeased,
contemplates through its yellow monocle
all that it now owns, blankly hating it.

A night out

Friends recommended the new Polish film
at the Academy in Oxford Street.
So we joined the ever melancholy queue
of cinemas. A wind blew faint suggestions
of rain towards us, and an accordion.
Later, uneasy, in the velvet dark
we peered through the cut-out oblong window
at the spotlit drama of our nightmares:
images of Auschwitz almost authentic,
the human obscenity in close-up.
Certainly we could imagine the stench.

Resenting it, we forgot the barbed wire
was but a prop, and could not scratch an eye:
those striped victims merely actors like us.
We saw the Camp orchestra assembled,
we heard the solemn gaiety of Bach,
scored by the loud arrival of an engine,
its impotent cry, and its guttural trucks.
We watched, as we munched milk chocolate,
trustful children, no older than our own,
strolling into the chambers without fuss,
whilst smoke, black and curly, oozed from chimneys.

Afterwards, at a loss, we sipped coffee
in a bored espresso bar nearby
saying very little. You took off one glove.
Then to the comfortable suburb swiftly
where, arriving home, we garaged the car.
We asked the au pair girl from Germany
if anyone had phoned at all, or called,
and, of course, if the children had woken.
Reassured, together we climbed the stairs,
undressed together, and naked together,
in the dark, in the marital bed, made love.

On the beach

HELEN: *I never went to Troy. Only a phantom went.*
MESSENGER: *What's this? All that suffering for nothing,*
    simply for a cloud?   [*Helena* Euripides]

Yawning, I fold yesterday's newspaper
from England, and its news of Vietnam
which has had, and will have, a thousand names.
Then I lie back on the tourist sand.

Between the sun and the sea,
far from the sun and nearer to the sea,
a cloud, a single cloud, perhaps
a cloud by Zeus planted,
not much higher than those mountains.
A cloud or a woman's face?

A cloud. Helen never came to Troy.
Mad Paris kissed the pillow where she was not,
straddled the phantom he thought he saw,
and soiling the sheets, lay back still jerking,
'Helen, Helen,' satisfied.

I rise. I am level with the haunted sea,
now clear and unclear too deep for wine,
that breathes, because of the cloud, in shadow.
It wrinkles gradually towards me.
Surprise—in the débris of near waves breaking,
deluded voices sound within its sound.

As if two, clad like Trojan women,
curse Helen—not sick Paris and his cloud.
For Hector is dead and this one is his mother,
for Hector is dead and that one is his wife,
and his babe, alive, is being torn by beasts.

No camera clicks, no front-page photograph,
no great interview. I laugh aloud,
and hear nearby a transistor braying.
Altered by its dance tune, wrongly I translate:
'Helen, Helen, where are you?
Except for that cloud the sky is blue.'

Later, I walk back to the hotel thinking:
wherever women crouch beside their dead,
as Hecuba did, as Andromache,
motionless as sculpture till they raise their head,
with mouths wildly open to howl and curse,
now they call that cloud not Helen, no,
but a thousand names, and each one still untrue.

Again I gaze beyond the mountains' range.
In depths below the sun the cloud floats through,
soundless, around the world, it seems, forever.
I go into the hotel, and change.

As I was saying

Yes, madam, as a poet I *do* take myself seriously,
and, since I have a young, questioning family, I suppose
I should know something about English wild flowers:
the shape of their leaves, when this and that one grows,
how old mythologies attribute strange powers
to this or that one. Urban, I should mug up anew
the pleasant names: Butterbur, Ling, and Lady's Smock,
Jack-by-the-Hedge, Cuckoo-Pint, and Feverfew,
even the Stinking Hellebore—all in that W. H. Smith book
I could bring home for myself (inscribed to my daughter)
to swot, to know which is this and which that one,
what honours the high cornfield, what the low water,
under the slow-pacing clouds and occasional sun
of England.
   But no! Done for in the ignorant suburb,
I'll drink Scotch, neurotically stare through glass
at the rainy lawn, at green stuff, nameless birds,
and let my daughter, madam, go to nature class.
I'll not compete with those nature poets you advance,
some in country dialect, and some in dialogue
with the country—few as calm as their words:
Wordsworth, Barnes, sad John Clare who ate grass.

Lady in distress

All this Victorian complaint of 'betrayed',
and 'vows broken'—somehow like the ribbon in your hair;
yet gazing into vulnerable eyes I fade
into silence. You have such an old-fashioned air.

Even your lace handkerchief, its decorous scent
of lavender, reminds of gentlewomen in hooped skirts;
perhaps bluff, hooting strangers would comment,
but because I do not, you appear more hurt.

Beauty dated, gilt framed, still you 'bare your heart',
unconsciously pose for a painting called Remorse.
I cannot, without offending you, depart. (Can not)
as you sigh about 'the children' and 'divorce'.

Dear, disinterested assertions are not wrong
only irrelevant as a lady's hat.
Pity, too, like a soft voice or loaded song
may confuse and confound, make a mock of it.

Some seem compassionate, some merely tough,
some cry, This is not love for love is not like this,
but since no man can ever know enough
all advice is prejudice.

Close up

Often you seem to be listening to a music
that others cannot hear. Rilke would have loved you:
you never intrude, you never ask questions
of those, crying in the dark, who are most near.

You always keep something of yourself to yourself
in the electric bars, even in bedrooms.
Rilke would have praised you: your nearness is far,
and, therefore, your distance like the very stars.

Yet some things you miss and some things you lose
by keeping your arm outstretched; and some things
you'll never know unless one, at least, knows you
like a close-up, in detail—blow by human blow.

Not Adlestrop

Not Adlestrop, no—besides, the name
hardly matters. Nor did I languish in June heat.
Simply, I stood, too early, on the empty platform,
and the wrong train came in slowly, surprised, stopped.
Directly facing me, from a window,
a very, *very* pretty girl leaned out.

    When I, all instinct,
stared at her, she, all instinct, inclined her head away
as if she'd divined the much married life in me,
or as if she might spot, up platform,
some unlikely familiar.

For my part, under the clock, I continued
my scrutiny with unmitigated pleasure.
And she knew it, she certainly knew it, and would not
glance at me in the silence of not Adlestrop.

    Only when the train heaved noisily, only
when it jolted, when it slid away, only *then*,
daring and secure, she smiled back at my smile,
and I, daring and secure, waved back at her waving.
And so it was, all the way down the hurrying platform
as the train gathered atrocious speed
towards Oxfordshire or Gloucestershire.

Olfactory pursuits

Often, unobserved, I smell my own hand.
I am searching for something forgotten.
I bang the door behind me, breathing in.

I think that a bitter or candied scent
is like a signpost pointing backwards
on which is writ no place and no distance.

So I walk towards a Verulamium,
your ruins or my ruins. The sun's ambushed:
fleeing on the ground the same, large shadow.

Look up. There's no smell to the colour blue.
The wind blew it right through the spaces
between clouds. Christ, what is it I'm after?

I dream, without sleeping, of things obscure,
of houses and streets and temples deserted
which, if once visited, I don't recall.

Here are a few stones instead of a wall,
and here broken stones instead of a house.
Hopelessly, with odours I conjoin.

My footfall echoes down old foundations,
buried mosaics, tomb tablets crumbled,
flints in the grass, your ruins or my ruins.

A man sniffs the back of his own hand,
moistens it with his mouth, to sniff again,
to think a blank; writes, 'The odour of stones'.

Halls

Halls of houses own a sweet biscuity smell;
and the carpet's frayed, the staircase lonely.

The landing light belongs to winter evenings.
When empty, all doors closed, the hall's itself.

It becomes an ear. Aware of a loud party
behind walls, and of cartilage clicking in a knee.

Between the porch and the head's eyes in a living room
it is the eight paces that can alter a man.

No wonder our grandfathers put clocks in halls,
and percussed barometers hopefully.

Lest the hall betray the host's formidable smile,
guests ushered in are not enticed to linger.

Later, guests leaving, slightly drunk, deranged,
neither know the hall nor the host, smileless.

What's detained by loitering, in gloomy halls,
near the leaded window and the telephone?

Well, nothing's defined by the keenest mind
aware of inviolate odours in halls.

Arcane, unparaphrasable halls.

In Llandough Hospital

'To hasten night would be humane,'
I, a doctor, beg a doctor,
for still the darkness will not come—
his sunset slow, his first star pain.

I plead: 'We know another law.
For one maimed bird we'd do as much,
and if a creature need not suffer
must he, for etiquette, endure?'

Earlier, 'Go now son', my father said,
for my sake commanding me.
Now, since death makes victims of us all,
he's thin as Auschwitz in that bed.

Still his courage startles me. The fears
I'd have, he has none. Who'd save
Socrates from the hemlock,
or Winkelried from the spears?

We quote or misquote in defeat,
in life, and at the camps of death.
Here comes the night with all its stars,
bright butchers' hooks for man and meat.

I grasp his hand so fine, so mild,
which still is warm surprisingly;
not a handshake either, father,
but as I used to when a child.

And as a child can't comprehend
what germinates philosophy,
so like a child I question why
night with stars, then night without end.

Interview with a spirit healer

Smiling, he says no man should fear the tomb
for where we fade the grass is greener.
Listen! Someone coughs in his waiting room;
then, from upstairs, the suburban howl of
the made ghost in a vacuum cleaner.

With nude emotion, he names the miracles
as hip fans would football matches.
His voice catches on the incurably cured
whose letters, testimonials, conclude,
'. . . though the doctors gave me up as hopeless'.

His tragic venue, those frayed English spas:
Cheltenham, Leamington, Tunbridge, Bath,
where depressed male Tories, on their sticks,
guzzle in chromium and maroon hotel bars
which seem more empty when people whisper.

He murmurs, 'Love', which could be disturbing,
also 'Spirit guides'. Look, his upraised hand
shows neither its knuckles nor its palm,
and, like a candle in daytime burning,
seems but a sign ethereal as a psalm.

Goodbye! His spirituality is too inbred,
too indelible like a watermark;
and I, gross sceptic, hired by a paper,
prefer my dead to be in the dark.
Goodbye. His eyes, Mary's blue, stare at vapour.

Let him, in faith, stare on. I loathe his trade,
the disease and the sanctimonious lie
that cannot cure the disease. My need,
being healthy, is not faith; but to curse the day
I became mortal the night my father died.

Pathology of colours

I know the colour rose, and it is lovely,
but not when it ripens in a tumour;
and healing greens, leaves and grass, so springlike,
in limbs that fester are not springlike.

I have seen red-blue tinged with hirsute mauve
in the plum-skin face of a suicide.
I have seen white, china white almost, stare
from behind the smashed windscreen of a car.

And the criminal, multi-coloured flash
of an H-bomb is no more beautiful
than an autopsy when the belly's opened—
to show cathedral windows never opened.

So in the simple blessing of a rainbow,
in the bevelled edge of a sunlit mirror,
I have seen, visible, Death's artifact
like a soldier's ribbon on a tunic tacked.

A winter convalescence

The coast shrugs, when the camera clicks,
deliberately. The cliffs blur,
and the sun's mashed in the west.

Its sac's broken, its egg-mess sticks
on the winter sea, smears it.
The air develops ghosts of soot
that become more evident, minute by minute.
They're clever. They have no shape.
Things hum.

Very few oblongs blaze
in the Grand Hotel.
God, how the promenade's empty.
The pier's empty too
but for the figure at the far end, shadowy,
hunched with a bending rod.
That one no taller than a thumb.

It's strange the way people go smaller
the further they are away. Most of the time
you even forget who died.
But supposing things did not get smaller?
Best to go inside. Best to push
revolving doors to where it's warmer,
where only a carpet makes you dizzy.

Inside, things hum.
Inside the insides the corridors wait.
A door opens, a hand comes out,
it's cut off at the elbow,
it holds a pair of shoes
cut off at the ankles.

Walk faster. God, someone is breathing,
walk faster. Humankind
cannot bear very much unreality.

That's right—lock this door, you clumsy . . .
Yet things still hum, things still hum.
Who blinks?
Who spies with his little eye
what no-one else has spied?
Best to pull the curtains on the night,
but then certain objects focus near:
the wardrobe with its narrow door,
the bible by the bedside.

Lie down, easy; lie down.
Who masturbated here?
Who whipped the ceilings? Cracked them?
Things hum.
Two blue, astringent eyes drag down their lids.
The dark comes from the lift-shaft.

Hunt the thimble

Hush now. You cannot describe it.

Is it like heavy rain falling,
and lights going on, across the fields,
in the new housing estate?

Cold, cold. Too domestic, too
temperate, too devoid of history.

Is it like a dark windowed street at night,
the houses uncurtained, the street deserted?

Colder. You are getting colder,
and too romantic, too dream-like.
You cannot describe it.

The brooding darkness then,
that breeds inside a cathedral
of a provincial town in Spain?

In Spain, also, but not Spanish.
In England, if you like, but not English.
It remains, even when obscure, perpetually.
Aged, but ageless, you cannot describe it.
No, you are cold, altogether too cold.

Aha—the blue sky over Ampourias,
the blue sky over Lancashire for that matter . . .

You cannot describe it.

. . . obscured by clouds?
I must know what you mean.

Hush, hush.

Like those old men in hospital dying,
who, unaware strangers stand around their bed,
stare obscurely, for a long moment,
at one of their own hands raised—
which perhaps is bigger than the moon again—
and then, drowsy, wandering, shout out, 'Mama'.

Is it like that? Or hours after that even:
the darkness inside a dead man's mouth?

No, no, I have told you:
you are cold, and you cannot describe it.

The smile was

one thing I waited for always
after the shouting
after the palaver
the perineum stretched to pain
the parched voice of the midwife
                    Push! Push!
and I can't, and the rank
sweet smell of the gas
and
                    I can't
as she whiffed cotton wool
inside her head
as the hollow stones of gas
dragged
            her
                down
from the lights above
to the river-bed, to the real stones.
                    Push! Push!
as she floated up again
muscles tensed, to the electric
till the little head was crowned;
and I shall wait again
for the affirmation.

For it is such:
that effulgent, tender, satisfied
smile of a woman
who, for the first time,
hears the child crying the world
for the very first time,
That agreeable, radiant smile—

no man can smile it
no man can paint it
as it develops without fail,
after the gross, physical, knotted,
granular, bloody endeavour.
　　Such a pure spirituality, from all that!
It occupies the face
and commands it.
　　　　　　Out of relief
you say, reasonably thinking of the reasonable,
swinging, lightness of any reprieve,
the joy of it, almost helium in the head.

　　　　　　So wouldn't you?
And truly there's always the torture of the unknown.
There's always the dream of pregnant women,
blood of the monster in the blood of the child;
and we all know of generations lost
like words faded on a stone,
of minds blank or wild with genetic mud.
　　　　　　And couldn't you
smile like that?

Not like that, no, never,
not with such indefinable
dulcitude as that.
And so she smiles
with eyes as brown as a dog's
or eyes blue-mad as a doll's
it makes no odds

whore, beauty, or bitch,
it makes no odds
illimitable chaste happiness
in that smile
as new life-in-the-world
for the first time cries the world.
No man can smile like that.

2

No man can paint it.
Da Vinci sought it out
yet was far, far, hopelessly.
Leonardo, you only made
Mona Lisa look six months gone!

I remember the smile of the Indian.
I told him
                    Fine, finished,
you are cured
and he sat there smiling sadly.
Any painter could paint it
the smile of a man resigned
saying
                    Thank you, doctor,
you have been kind
and then, as in melodrama,
                    How long
have I to live?
The Indian smiling, resigned,
all the fatalism of the East.

So one starts again, also smiling,
                    All is well

you are well, you are cured.
and the Indian still smiling
his assignations with death
still shaking his head, resigned.
                    Thank you
for telling me the truth, doctor.
Two months? Three months?

And beginning again
    and again
whatever I said, thumping the table,
however much I reassured him
the more he smiled the conspiratorial
smile of a damned, doomed man.

Now a woman, a lady, a whore,
a bitch, a beauty, whatever,
    the child's face crumpled,
as she becomes the mother
she smiles differently, ineffably.

3

As different as
the smile of my colleague,
his eyes reveal it,
his ambiguous assignations,
good man, good surgeon,
whose smile arrives of its own accord
    from nowhere
like flies to a dead thing
when he makes the first incision.

Who draws a line of blood
across the soft, white flesh
as if something beneath,
desiring violence, had beckoned him;
who draws a ritual wound,
a calculated wound
to heal—to heal,
but still a wound—
good man, good surgeon,
his smile as luxuriant
as the smile of Peter Lorre.

So is the smile of my colleague,
the smile of a man
secretive behind the mask.

The smile of war.

But the smile, the smile
of the new mother,
what
        an extraordinary
            open thing
                    it is.

4

Walking home tonight I saw
an ordinary occurrence
hardly worth remarking on:
an unhinged star, a streaking gas,
and I thought how lovely

destruction is when it is far.
Ruined it slid
on the dead dark towards fiction:
its lit world disappeared
phut, through one punched hole or another,
slipped unseen down the back of the sky
into another time.

Never,
not for one single death
can I forget we die with the dead,
and the world dies with us;
yet
in one, lonely,
small child's birth
all the tall dead rise
to break the crust of the imperative earth.

No wonder the mother smiles
a wonder like that,
a lady, a whore, a bitch, a beauty.
Eve smiled like that
when she heard Seth cry out Abel's dark,
earth dark, the first dark
eeling on the deep sea-bed,
struggling on the real stones.
Hecuba, Cleopatra, Lucretia Borgia,
Annette Vallon smiled like that.

They all, still, smile like that,
when the child first whimpers like a seagull
the ancient smile reasserts itself

instinct with a return
so outrageous and so shameless;
the smile the smile
always the same
                an uncaging
                        a freedom.